For my father, Marshal A. Perkins,

who never wrote this letter to me, but who taught me all the things that should go in it, and who taught me everything I know about being a dad.

Dear Austin

A Letter To My Son

David M. Perkins

From the Author

It comes to pass, in every parent's life, that a child will begin preparations to leave home. Some will be off to college, some will go to the military or other national service, and many will just strike out to seek their fortunes in whatever field has captured their imagination.

It's at this moment, when the preparation begins, that most parents will realize that all those heart-to-heart talks they always intended to have with their offspring somehow never took place. Or, at the very least, that many of them managed to slip through the cracks.

It was in this environment of not-quite-panic that I sat down at my computer to make up for missed opportunities. I had no idea what I was going to say to my son, but I knew I had to say *something*.

The eventual letter, which follows, came as something of a surprise to me. Not right away, but later, as I'll explain. And the chance sharing of this letter with a friend, at a similar place in life, resulted in me being encouraged to share it with others. Thank you, Lia.

After installing my son in his college dorm, and leaving the letter with him, my wife and I spent a very quiet five hours driving back home. I guess we were both lost in our own thoughts about the past, the future, and the somewhat less than action-packed present.

When we arrived home, I went to my office and read the letter again, to myself. Several times, I confess. This is when I had my *epiphany*. I've never had one before, but I'm pretty sure that's what it was.

I concluded that my subconscious had tricked me into writing what I believed were things my son needed to hear; about me, about life, and about his future. And while I still hope that he may find something of value in it, I came to realize that I had actually written things that *I* needed to know; about *him*, about *his* life, and about our relationship. I was writing to me, as much as to him. Not all of it, of course, but just enough to reassure myself that he would be alright.

This awareness allowed me to suddenly let go of some of the sadness about his leaving, and to replace it with some of the hope and excitement that he must be feeling now. It is in this spirit, and with my son's permission, that I share this letter with any parent who has lost, or will lose, a child to higher education, or military service, or to the most dreaded thief of all, adulthood.

David M. Perkins
April 2010

Dear Austin

A Letter To My Son

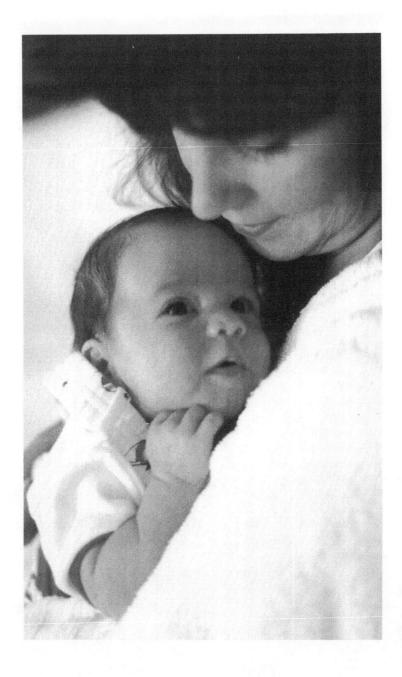

Dear Austin—

I've been thinking about this letter for weeks now, and I still don't really know what I'm going to write. I know there are things I need to say to you, things I want you to know, but I'll be damned if I can figure out what should come first. So, forgive me for rambling.

It's difficult to watch you get ready to leave home. You have been nothing but a source of pride for your mother and me for your entire life, and we're delighted to see you begin the next chapter, and move on to bigger and better and more exciting things. Life is really just beginning for you, and it's exhilarating, and frightening, and promising all at once. But it's hard, too, for us.

Even though you're not leaving home for good, and you'll still be here a lot over the next few years, it will be different. You really are a young man now, and our relationship with you will never be the same. That's okay. It's not *supposed* to be the same. But, for your mom and me, it will be a bittersweet transition.

You will miss it

You should know, ahead of time, that even when you're forty and your mom is seventy-seven, you will still be her little boy. She will still worry that you're getting enough to eat, that you're keeping warm enough, and that you're safe. She will still be a pain in the ass. As long as she lives, that will never go away. And when it finally does, you will miss it.

You will also be my little boy for as long as I live, and the memory of you falling asleep on my chest warms me even now. But ours will evolve into a man to man friendship, where I am less an authority figure and more of a friend, and it will get stronger as time passes. Exactly how our relationship will change will take some time to find itself, and there might be occasions when it feels awkward, but we will find our place in each other's lives, and it will be comfortable and good. And, yes, I will still be a pain in the ass.

*We will find our place
in each other's lives*

Never fear the consequences of honesty between the two of us.

All of that said, I will always be your dad first. I will always be there if you need advice, or comfort, or a shoulder to cry on, or just someone to share news with – good or bad.

It's possible that you might someday disappoint me, or I you. People sometimes disappoint those they love. But there is nothing you can do that could ever cause me to stop loving you. There is no conversation we cannot have. Never fear the consequences of honesty between the two of us.

I won't spend a lot of time urging you to study hard and do well in school. You're smart enough to realize that, if you're going to have the opportunity to continue your college education, you must maintain an acceptable level of accomplishment; acceptable both to the school and to your mom and me. Anything less will be a waste of your time and money, and will result in a future that is much less than you dream of. Don't squander the possibility of this moment.

Don't squander
the possibility of
this moment.

The next few years are a time for you to discover *who* you are, and *what* you are, and what you believe. Your mother and I have given you the values and beliefs that we think are worthwhile, and they should be helpful to you as you begin your own search. But ultimately you will have to decide if they have a place in your life; if they are really *your* values and beliefs.

It's a time to discover who you are and what you are

Everyone must find his own truth. My father was the most honorable and honest man I've ever known, but some of my truths didn't fully square with his, and some of yours won't square with mine. Don't ever let that stop you from pursuing them. It doesn't make either of us wrong.

*Everyone must find
his own truth.*

Chase your dreams ...

Not mine

It seems a natural affliction that children want to make their parents proud. It's understandable, and commendable, to a point. But in seeking to please someone else, you can be diverted into pursuing goals that are not your own. Chase *your* dreams, not mine, nor your mother's, nor anyone else's whose respect you desire. If you can't gain someone's approval by being true to yourself, then it's approval that you can survive without.

The temptation to experiment with dangerous things will be great, and I wish I could find words that would effectively dissuade you from considering them. But I won't try. No father has ever protected a son from his own mistakes. I will only implore you not to risk your health or life, nor the health or lives of others. Make every effort to exercise discretion when choosing what to try, when and where to try it, and with whom. And be aware of the possible legal, moral, academic, and career implications of any behavior you consider engaging in.

No father has ever
protected a son from his
own mistakes.

Experiment carefully

You know that I have no problem with the responsible use of alcohol, but in deciding whether or not it has a place in your lifestyle, keep one eye on your family history. I know that you already know that your family is littered, on both sides, with alcoholics, many of whom literally drank themselves to death. Others died of "natural causes" that might never have happened but for alcohol abuse.

It is entirely possible that you are genetically predisposed to alcohol or drug addiction. It is not a character flaw. It is not a lack of will. It is a disease, and you may not know if you're susceptible until it's out of your control. If you choose to use alcohol, experiment carefully, and pay attention to how your mind and your body react to its effects.

Don't get caught up in the chase for money. There's nothing wrong with money, in and of itself, and wanting and having nice "things" is perfectly natural. But the pursuit of money and things can cause you to lose sight of what is truly good and important in life. Don't let that become your story.

Instead, pursue the *life* that you want to live, and let that pursuit be led by what you truly love. Find your passion and try to build your life around it. Everything good will come from that. You may never be wealthy, but if you spend your life at something you love, and surround yourself with people who care about you, you will be light years ahead of almost everyone else in the pursuit of happiness.

Find your passion

Be open. Be curious.

You're a handsome young man. You're funny. You're talented. And people like to be around you. It would be easy for you to try to coast through life on those traits alone. Avoid the temptation to do that. Make a conscious decision *not* to do that. While it might afford you a pleasant enough life, it will rob it of passion and meaning and success, no matter how you choose to measure it.

Try, always, to treat others with respect and dignity, no matter who they are or how little you feel they deserve it. Go out of your way to meet, and have conversations with, those with whom you have little in common. Spend time talking with people who disagree with your points of view. Expose yourself to things you know little about.

Be open. Be curious. This next few years are when you will *become* you. Don't miss an opportunity to discover something you might love that could lead to a more complete, more fulfilled, and more accomplished you.

Don't cling too doggedly to your beliefs *just because they're your beliefs*. Always be willing to entertain the possibility that some tenet you've long held dear has been wrong. It happens. Just as importantly, don't surrender them when you *know* you're right.

As much as you love music, as much as we *both* love music, I am reluctant to encourage you to pursue it as a career unless you just can't see yourself doing anything else. You have to want that above all else, and even then it will likely be a financially difficult life. If you know that, and are prepared for it, then it can still be an enormously happy and satisfying life. Look at the people you know personally who have chosen this path, and how they've made it work for them. If you can see yourself teaching, or repairing instruments, or even building them, or any of the hundreds of jobs you can do in the field of music, and you can be content doing those things, then go for it.

If you choose another field for a career, try not to let a day go by without picking up an instrument. Your life will be richer, calmer, less discouraging, and more at ease with music in it. It can rescue you from the darkest places. Keep it with you always, and pass it on to your children.

Keep music with you always,
and pass it on to your
children.

Never be afraid to fail

Never be afraid to fail. *Please* fail. I know this goes against everything you've been taught up to now, but if you never fail in your life it only means that you've never tried to do anything worthwhile. Never let the fear of looking foolish, or inept, keep you from attempting something scary. If you only allow yourself to look foolish on your own terms, you will miss out on some wondrous opportunities.

Treat women well

Treat women well. Despite their protests to the contrary, they still like to be regarded as special. And they are. Never mislead about your intentions, or your feelings, even if it costs you an opportunity to be with someone you're really attracted to. The number of your conquests is not a measure of your manhood; your *stamina* maybe, but not your manhood.

I won't pretend that sex in a casual encounter cannot be satisfying. But, when engaged in with the right person at the right time, it can be emotionally and spiritually nourishing as well. I don't mean to go all nineteenth century on you, and I'm not saying that true love is a requisite. I *am* saying that an emotional connection, on some level, with your partner will make it more fulfilling for you both. As difficult as it might be some of the time, try to give some thought to the quality of your sex life, rather than the quantity alone. It should be more than a temporary indulgence of hormonally driven appetites. Allow it to *mean* something.

One day, sooner or later, your heart will be broken. If I could protect you from one thing, it would be this. But I can't. You will feel as though you can't go on; that the pain will never go away, and that you will never love anyone, ever, again. But it will. And you will. If you trust anything I say to you, trust this: you *will* be okay.

You will be okay

*I will leave a paper trail
for that day when you
start to wonder.*

I often wonder what my dad would have thought, or done, in a particular set of circumstances. Sometimes I think I know, and other times I'm not sure. I have tried, and will continue, to leave a paper trail for you.

When you're young, you don't much give a damn about what your parents think. But one day you will, and it might not be possible to ask. So I will leave as much for you as I can for that day when you start to wonder.

Your entire life is going to be about choices; superb ones, and poor ones, but mostly the ones that fall somewhere in between. They will all have consequences; some good, some bad, some hardly noticeable. Some will have minimal effect on your life. Some will bring new understanding. Some will be life altering, and some could be tragic, or even deadly.

But however they turn out, *you are responsible for the choices you make.* Own them. Be proud of them, when appropriate. Learn from them when you can. Apologize for them if the situation demands. But don't *ever* deny them. They are yours, for better or worse.

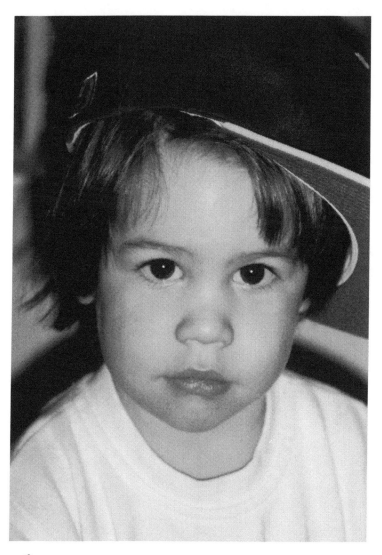

You are responsible for the choices you make

Try your best

to contribute

The world *is* yours. And I apologize from the bottom of my heart for giving it to you in such miserable condition. It's now up to you, and your generation, and your children's generation, to repair what we have done to it. Try your best to contribute. Do what you can to leave it better for your children than I have left it for you. I'm afraid that my generation has been criminally negligent, and you will have to pay the price.

Finally, be a good friend. You'll be lucky if, during your lifetime, you have three or four truly good friends. The ones you'll trust with your life, or even your child's life. You know, the ones who'll help you move bodies. Don't let those go without very good reason, and certainly don't allow them to just slip away.

Be as good a friend to these people as they are to you. A real friendship can't be one-sided. It requires active concern, and regard, and participation on both sides, or it will simply dry up and blow away.

Be a good friend

*I want you to be
a happy person*

If you'll spend at least as much time trying to figure out how you can serve the needs of others as you do trying to serve your own, your life will be richer and fuller and much more satisfying.

You know that I'm not a religious man. But I *do* believe that we are all connected, and the more we do for each other, the more we do for ourselves. You *cannot* spend your life in pursuit of self-satisfaction alone and be a truly happy person. And more than anything else in this world, I *want* you to be a happy person.

I love you. I wish you only joy and success, however you choose to define it. Just do your best to be open, and to recognize it when it comes.

Dad

Acknowledgments

I would like to thank my wife, Ryan, for being the "pain in the ass" mom that resulted in such a great kid, and made the job of being the dad so much fun.

Thanks to my son, Austin, for his permission to make this letter public, and for making fatherhood such a joy. And thank you for inspiring some of my better prose.

Thanks to my dear friend, Lia Carmody, for suggesting that this might be a book. Thanks also for her wonderful photographs, documenting our lives over the years, many of which are included here.

And a special thank you to Carl Bluemel for his time, talent, and expertise in designing and laying out this book for publication. You rock!

Photographs by:

Lia Carmody, Ryan Perkins, DiAnne Perkins, and me.

Contact:

DiAnne Perkins –
www.yourplaceorminephoto.com

Carl Bluemel –
www.bluemelcreative.com

About the Author

David M. Perkins has spent the past thirty years as a telecine colorist in the motion picture and television industry in Los Angeles. He is a writer, and a long time member of the Writers Guild of America, west. But mostly, he's a father and a husband.

He currently lives, with his wife and son, in Southern California and devotes much of his time to building and maintaining internet websites.

You can learn more about him, and his writing, at
www.davidmperkins.com
or contact him by email at
david@davidmperkins.com.

This book is available at *www.davidmperkins.com* and other book retailers, online and off.

Made in the USA
Charleston, SC
07 April 2013